Animal Peculiarity Part 4

By T.P Just

~~~

Copyright © 2010 by Terence Just. All rights reserved.

I0436063

Get All The Books In The Series:

Table of Contents

1 Prologue

THERE is perhaps nothing extraordinary in the fact that man is wise and just, takes great care to provide for his own children, -shows due consideration for his parents, seeks sustenance for himself, protects himself against plots, and possesses all the other gifts of nature which are his. For man has been endowed with speech, of all things the most precious, and has been granted reason, which is of the greatest help and use.

Moreover, he knows how to reverence and worship the gods. But that dumb animals should by nature possess some good quality and should have many of man's amazing excellences assigned to them along with man, is indeed a remarkable fact. And to know accurately the special characteristics of each, and how living creatures also have been a source of interest no less than man, demands a trained intelligence and much learning. Now I am well aware of the labour that others have expended on this subject, yet I have collected all the materials that I could; I have clothed them in untechnical language, and am persuaded that my achievement is a treasure far from negligible. So if anyone considers them profitable, let him make use of them; anyone who does not consider them so may give them to his father to keep and attend to.

For not all things give pleasure to all men, nor do all men consider all subjects worthy of study. Although I was born later than many accomplished writers of an earlier day, the accident of date ought not to mulct me of praise, if I too produce a learned work whose ampler research and whose choice of language make it deserving of serious attention.

Mythology, mariners' yarns, vulgar superstitions, the ascertained facts of nature—all serve to adorn a tale and, on occasion, to point a moral. His religion is the popular stoicism of the age. Aleian repeatedly affirms his belief in the gods and in divine providence; the wisdom and beneficence of Nature are held up to veneration; the folly and selfishness of man are contrasted with the untaught virtues of the animal world. Some animals, to be sure, have their failings, but he chooses rather to dwell upon their good qualities, devotion, courage, self-sacrifice, gratitude. Again, animals are guided by reason, and from them we may learn contentment, control of the passions, and calm in the face of death.

2 The Cerastes

The Cerastes is a small creature; it is a snake, and above its brow it has two horns, and these horns are like those of the snail, though unlike the snail's they are not soft.

And the Psylli

Now these snakes are the enemies of all other Libyans, but towards the Psylli, as they are called, they are gently disposed, for the Psylli are insensible to their bites and have no difficulty in curing those who have fallen victims to this venomous creature.

Their method is this: if one of that tribe arrive, whether summoned or by chance, before the whole body is inflamed, and if he then rinse his mouth with water and wash the bitten man's hands and give him the water from both to drink, then the victim recovers and thereafter is free from all infection.

And there is a story current among the Libyans that, if one of the Psylli suspects his wife and hates her on the ground that she has committed adultery; and if moreover he suspects that the child born from her is a bastard and no true member of his tribe, he then puts it to a very severe test: he fills a chest with Cerastae and drops the baby among them, just as a goldsmith places gold in the fire, and puts the infant to the proof by thus exposing him.

And immediately the snakes surge up in anger and threaten the child with their native poison. But directly the infant touches them, they wilt, and then the Libyan knows that he is the father of no bastard but of one sprung of his own race. This tribe is said also to be the enemy of other noxious beasts and of malmignattes.

Well, if the Libyans are here romancing, I would have them know that it is not I but themselves that they are deceiving.

3 Bees and their enemies

The following creatures plot and make war against Bees: the creatures known as Titmice and their young, also Wasps and Swallows and Snakes and Spiders and [Moths?]. Bees are afraid of these, and so bee-keepers try to drive them away by using fleabane as a fumigant or by placing or scattering poppies still green before the hives.

Most of the aforesaid creatures dislike these things, but the way to catch Wasps is as follows. You should hang up a cage in front of the Wasps' nest and insert a little a smelt or a small sprat and with them a minnow or, a sardine. And the Wasps, drawn by their natural greed and lured by the bait, fall into the cage in numbers, and once they are trapped, it is no longer possible for them to fly out again.

Lizards also have designs upon a Bee, so too have Land-crocodiles. But a means has been devised of destroying them too, thus: soak some meal in hellebore, or pour upon it the sap of spurge or the juice of mallow and scatter it about in front of the hives. This is death to the aforesaid creatures, once they have tasted.-of it.

If a bee-keeper drops the leaves of mullein or nuts into a pool, he will find it the simplest way of destroying Tadpoles. But Moths are destroyed at nighttime by the placing of a strong light in front of the hives and vessels full of oil below the light. And the Moths fly to the brightness and fall into the oil and are killed, otherwise they would not be caught so very easily. But the Titmice, once they have tasted the wine-steeped meal, become drowsy; then they fall over and lie quivering and can readily (?) be captured as they struggle to fly and are quite incapable of standing. But the Swallow men refrain from killing out of respect for its music, though they might easily do so.

They are content to hinder the Swallow from attaching its nest below the hives. Again, Bees dislike all bad smells and perfume, equally they cannot endure foul odors nor do they welcome a luxurious fragrance, even as modest, refined girls abhor the former while despising the latter.

4. Bees, their combs and hives

The elder Cyrus, they say, was filled with pride at the palace in Persepolis which he himself had caused to be built; Darius likewise at the magnificence of his buildings at Susa, for he it was who contrived those far-famed dwelling-places.

Cyrus the Second with his own royal hands and clothed in his habitual delicate garments and adorned with his beautiful jewels of great price, planted his Gardens in Lydia and prided himself on the fact before all the Greeks and even before Lysander the Spartan, when Lysander came to visit him in Lydia.

Historians celebrate these constructions, but the dwellings of Bees which are far cleverer and exhibit a greater skill; of these they take not the slightest notice. And yet, while those monarchs wrought what they wrought through the affliction of multitudes, there never was any creature more gracious than the Bee, just as there is none cleverer.

The first things that they construct are the chambers of their kings, and they are spacious and above all the rest. Round them they put a barrier, as it were a wall or fence, thereby also enhancing the importance of the royal dwelling.

And they divide themselves into three grades, and their dwellings accordingly into the same number. Thus, the eldest dwell nearest the royal palace, and the latest born dwell next to them, while those that are young and in the prime of life are outside the latter. In this way the eldest are the king's bodyguard, and the youthful ones are a protection to the latest born.

5 The King Bee

According to one story the King Bees are stingless; according to another they are born with stings of great strength and trenchant sharpness; and yet they never use them against a man nor against bees: the stings are a pretence, an empty scare, for it would be wrong for one who rules and directs such numbers to do an injury.

And those who understand their ways bear witness to the fact that the other Bees when in presence of their rulers withdraw their stings, as though shrinking and giving way before authority. And one might well be astonished at either of the aforesaid characteristics in these King Bees: if they have no means of injuring, this is remarkable; if with all the means of injuring they do no injury, then this is far more to their credit.

6The Migration Of Cranes

When Cranes are about to leave their Thracian haunts and the frosts of Thrace, they collect on the river, Hebrus and when each one has swallowed a stone by way of food and as ballast against the on on-slaught of winds, they prepare to emigrate and to set out for the Nile, longing for the warmth and for the food that is to be had there during the winter.

And just when they are on the point of rising and moving off, the oldest Crane goes round the entire a flock thrice and then falls to the ground and breathes his last. So the others bury the dead body on the spot and fly straight to Egypt, traversing the widest seas on outstretched wing, never landing, and never pausing to rest.

And they fall in with the Egyptians as they are sowing their fields, and in the plough lands they find, so to speak, a generous table, and though uninvited partake of the Egyptians' hospitality.

7 Fire-flies

That living creatures should be born upon the mountains, in the air, and in the sea, is no great marvel, since matter, food, and nature are the cause. But that there should spring from fire winged creatures which men call 'Fire-flies' and that these should live and flourish in it, flying to and fro about it, is a startling fact.

And what is more extra- ordinary, when these creatures stray outside the range of the-heat to which they are accustomed and take in cold air, they at once perish. And why they should be born in the fire and die in the air others must explain.

8 Swallows and their mating

With other birds the hen is mounted by the cock, so they say;
not so swallows: their manner of coupling is the reverse.
Nature alone knows the reason for this. But the common
explanation is that the hens are afraid of Tereus, and fear lest
one day he steal secretly upon them and enact a fresh tragedy.
Now in my opinion the most valuable gift that nature has
bestowed upon the Swallow is this, that if it chance to be
blinded with a brooch-pin, it regains its sight. Why then do we
continue to sing the praises of a Teiresias, even though he was
the wisest of men not only on earth but also in Hades, as
Homer tells us.

9 The Basilisk and other snakes

Archelaus tells us that in Libya mules that have been wounded or which have succumbed from thirst are thrown out for dead in great numbers. And frequently a multitude of snakes of all kinds comes streaming up to eat their flesh. But whenever they hear the hiss of the Basilisk they disappear as swiftly as possible into their dens or beneath the sand, and hide ;so the Basilisk on reaching the spot feasts in complete tranquility. Then again with a hiss he is off, and thereafter as to the mules and to the feast which they provide, 'he marks their place,' as the saying has it, 'only by the stars.

'Ephemera'

There are creatures called Ephemera (living only for a day) that take their name from their span of life, for they are generated in wine, and when the vessel is opened they fly out, see the light, and die. Thus it is that Nature has permitted them to come to life, but has rescued them as soon as possible from life's evils, so that they are neither aware of their own misfortune nor are spectators of the misfortune of others.

The Asp, its bite

Men have, it is true, recovered after a long while from the bite of an Asp, either by summoning excision to their aid or with the utmost fortitude enduring cautery, or they have in their plight pre- vented the poison from spreading, by taking the necessary medicines.

The Basilisk

The Basilisk measures but a span, yet at the sight of it the longest snake not after an interval but on the instant, at the mere impact of its breath, shrivels. And if a man has a stick in his hand and the Basilisk bites it, the owner of the rod dies.

10 Fisherman and Dolphins

There are stories which reach us from Euboea of fisher-folk in those parts sharing their catch equally with the Dolphins in those parts. And I am told that they fish in this way. The weather must be calm, and if it is, they attach to the prow of their boats some hollow braziers with fire burning in them, and one can see through them, so that while retaining the fire they do not conceal the light.

They call them lanterns. Now the fish are afraid of the brightness and are dazzled by the glare and some of them not knowing what is the- purpose of the thing they see, draw near from a wish to discover what it is that frightens them.

Then terror-stricken they either lie still in a mass close to some rock, quivering with fear, or are cast ashore as they are jostled along, and seem thunderstruck. Of course in that condition it is perfectly easy to harpoon them.

So when the Dolphins observe that the fishermen have lit their fire, they get ready to act, and while the men row softly the Dolphins scare the fish on the outskirts and push them and prevent any escape.

Accordingly the fish pressed on all sides and in some degree surrounded, realise that there is no escaping from the men that row and the Dolphins that swim; so they remain where they are and are caught in great numbers. And the Dolphins approach as though demanding the profits of their common labor due to them from this store of food.

And the fishermen loyally and gratefully resign to their comrades in the chase their just portion-assuming that they wish them to come again, unsummoned and prompt, to their aid, for those toilers of the sea are convinced that if they omit to do this, they will make enemies of those who were once friends.

11 Deer and Snakes

A Deer defeats a snake by an extraordinary gift that Nature has bestowed. And the fiercest snake lying in its den cannot escape, but the Deer applies its nostrils to the spot where the venomous creature lurks, breathes into it with the utmost force, attracts it by the spell, as it- were, of its breath, draws it forth against its will, and when it peeps out, begins to eat it. Especially in the winter does it do this. Indeed it has even happened that a man has ground a Deer's horn to powder and then has thrown the powder into fire, and that the mounting smoke has driven the snakes from the entire neighborhood: even the smell is to them unendurable.

12 Mare and Ass

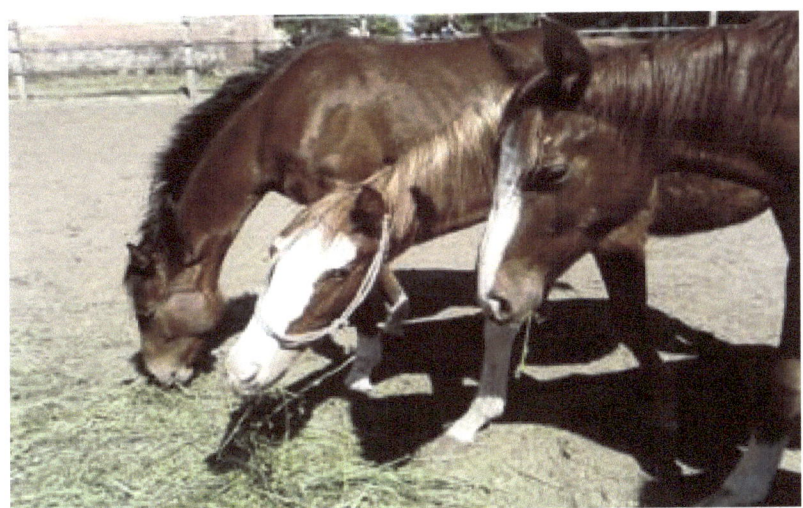

The Horse is generally speaking a proud creature, the reason being that his size, his speed, his tall neck, the suppleness of his limbs, and the clang of his hooves make him insolent and vain. But it is chiefly a Mare with a long mane that is so full of airs and graces.

For instance, she scorns to be covered by an ass, but is glad to mate with a horse, regarding herself as only fit for the greatest (of her kind). Accordingly those who wish to have mules born, knowing this characteristic, clip the Mare's mane in a haphazard fashion anyhow, and then put asses to her.

Though ashamed at first, she admits her present ignoble mate. Sophocles also appears to mention this humiliation.

13 The Elephant, its docility

Touching the sagacity of Elephants I have spoken elsewhere; and further, I have spoken too of the manner of hunting them, mentioning but a few of the numerous facts recorded by others. For the present I intend to speak of their sense for music and their readiness to obey and their aptitude for learning things which are difficult even for mankind, to say nothing of so huge an animal and one hitherto so fierce to encounter.

The movements of a chorus, the steps of a dance, how to march in time, how to enjoy the sound of flutes, how to distinguish different notes, when to slacken pace as permitted or when to quicken at command-all these things the Elephant has learnt and knows how to do, and does accurately without making mistakes.

Thus, while nature has created him to be the largest of animals, learning has rendered him the most gentle and docile. Now had I set out to write about the readiness to obey and to learn among elephants in India or in Ethiopia or in Libya, anyone might suppose that I was concocting some pretentious tale, that in fact I was on the strength of hearsay about the beast giving a completely false account of its nature. That is the last thing that a man in pursuit of knowledge and an ardent lover of the truth has any right to do. Instead I have preferred to state what I have myself seen and what others have recorded as having formerly occurred in Rome, treating summarily a few facts out of many, which in nevertheless sufficiently demonstrate the peculiar nature of the beast.

14 Performing Elephants In Rome

The Elephant when once tamed is the gentlest of resuming creatures and is easily induced to do whatever one wants. Now keeping due eye on the time, I shall state the most important events first. Germanicus Caesar was about to give some shows for the Romans. (He would be the nephew of Tiberius.).

There were in Rome several full-grown male and female elephants, and there were calves born of them in the country; and when their limbs began to grow firm, a man who was clever at dealing with such beasts trained them and instructed them with uncanny and astounding dexterity.

To begin with he introduced them in a quiet, gentle fashion to his instructions, supplying them with delicacies and the most appetizing food, varied so as to allure and entice them into abandoning all trace of ferocity and into becoming renegades, that is tame and to some degree human.

So what they learnt was not to go wild at the sound of flutes, not to be alarmed at the beating of drums, to be charmed by the pipe and to endure discordant notes, the beat of marching feet, and the singing of crowds. Moreover they were thoroughly trained not to be afraid of men in masses. And further their disciplining was manly in the following respects: they were not to get angry at the infliction of a blow, nor, when obliged to move some limb and to sway in time to dance or song, to burst into; a rage, even though they had attained to such strength and courage.

Now to refrain by instinct from misbehaving and from flouting the instruction given by a man is a virtue and a mark of nobility. When therefore the dancing- master had brought them to a high degree of proficiency, and they performed accurately what he had taught them, they did not disappoint the labour spent on their training (so they say) in the place where in due time the occasion demanded that they should display what they had been taught.

Now this troupe was twelve in number, and they advanced in two groups from the right and the left sides of the theatre. They entered with a mincing gait, swaying their whole body in a delicate manner, and they were clothed in the flowered garments of dancers. And at no more than a word from the conductor they formed into line (so we are told) — supposing that to have been their teacher's order.

Then again they wheeled into a circle when he so ordered them, and if they had to deploy, that also they did. And then they sprinkled flowers to deck the floor, but with moderation and economy, and now and again they stamped, keeping time in a rhythmical dance.

That Damon therefore, that Spintharus, Aristoxenus, Philoxenus, and others should be experts in music and should be numbered among the few for their knowledge of it is certainly matter for wonder but by no means incredible or absurd. The reason is that man is a rational animal capable of understanding and logical thought.

But that an inarticulate animal should comprehend rhythm and melody, should follow the movements of a tragic dance without a false step, fulfilling all that its lessons required of it- these are gifts bestowed by Nature, and each, one is a singularity that fills one with amazement.

Elephants at a banquet

But what followed was enough to send the spectator wild with delight. On the sand of the theatre at were placed mattresses of low couches, and on these in turn cushions, and over them embroidered coverlets, clear evidence of a house of great prosperity and ancestral wealth.

And close at hand were set costly goblets and bowls of gold and of silver, and in them a large quantity of water; and beside them were placed tables of citrus wood and of ivory, of great magnificence, and they were laden with meat and bread enough to satisfy the stomachs of the most voracious animals. So as soon as the preparations were completed in all their abundance, the banqueters came on, six males and an equal number of females; the former were clad in masculine garb, the latter in feminine; and they took their places in orderly fashion in pairs, a male and a female. And at a signal they reached forward their trunks modestly, as though they were hands, and ate with great decorum.

And not one of them gave the impression of being a glutton nor yet of trying to forestall others or of being inclined to snatch too large a portion, as the Persian did who occurs in Xenophon the golden. And when they wanted to drink, a bowl was placed by each one, from which they sucked up the water with their trunks and drank it in an orderly manner, and then proceeded to squirt (the attendants) 6 in fun, not by way of insult.

Many similar stories have been recorded showing the astounding ingenuity of these animals. And I myself have seen one actually with its trunk writing Roman letters on a tablet in a straight line without any deviation.

The only thing was that the instructor's hand was laid upon it, directing it to the shape of the letters until the animal had finished writing; and it looked intently down. You would have said that the animal's eyes had been taught and knew the letters.

Get All The Books In The Series:

Animal Peculiarity Part 1
Animal Peculiarity Part 2
Animal Peculiarity part 3
Animal Peculiarity Part 4
Animal Peculiarity Part 5
Animal Peculiarity Part 6
Animal Peculiarity Part 7
Animal Peculiarity Part 8

www.ingramcontent.com/pod-product-compliance
Lightning Source LLC
Chambersburg PA
CBHW050922290526
45792CB00002B/853